LANCASHIRE
IN PHOTOGRAPHS

JON SPARKS

AMBERLEY

First published 2017

Amberley Publishing
The Hill, Stroud
Gloucestershire, GL5 4EP

www.amberley-books.com

Copyright © Jon Sparks, 2017

The right of Jon Sparks to be identified as the Author of this work has been
asserted in accordance with the Copyrights, Designs and Patents Act 1988.

ISBN 978 1 4456 6730 0 (print)
ISBN 978 1 4456 6731 7 (ebook)

British Library Cataloguing in Publication Data.
A catalogue record for this book is available from the British Library.

Origination by Amberley Publishing.
Printed in the UK.

ABOUT THE PHOTOGRAPHER

Jon Sparks is a freelance photographer and writer specialising in the outdoors. He's been based in Lancashire all his working life, and founded his professional career on images of the county and adjoining areas. While he's had fantastic experiences in New Zealand, Pakistan, Jordan and other far-flung spots, many of his favourite places are much closer to home. Jon now lives in Garstang and counts himself lucky to have the Forest of Bowland on his doorstep.

Alongside pure landscape photography, he's worked extensively on outdoor pursuits; in fact he'd argue that there's no hard boundary between the two. He's tried most activities but has a special love of all things bike-related, whether skinny-tyred road bikes or mountain bikes. He's also a lifelong hill walker, scrambler and 'resting' rock climber. He's picked up awards for both writing and photography, and indeed has written extensively about photography.

INTRODUCTION

Photographing Lancashire has been an important part of my professional life for over twenty-five years, and I was doing it as an amateur long before that – there must be something about the place that keeps me going.

There's plenty of landscape quality, for a start. Lancashire has a half-share in one Area of Outstanding Natural Beauty (AONB) – Arnside-Silverdale – and the lion's share of another, the Forest of Bowland. Since the extension of National Park boundaries in 2016, it also has a toehold in the Yorkshire Dales National Park. There are many other cherished areas too; for example, a large swathe of the West Pennine Moors recently became the largest new Site of Special Scientific Interest created since 2004. Inevitably, the selection of photos leans heavily on these noted areas, but there's plenty more to enjoy.

Another factor that helps keep me fresh is exploring Lancashire in a range of different ways. Walking is always a natural complement to landscape photography, of course, but I've gained different and equally valuable perspectives from both road and mountain bikes. As Ernest Hemingway said, 'It is by riding a bicycle that you learn the contours of a country best, since you have to sweat up the hills and coast down them.' Rock climbing and the odd bit of ghyll-scrambling have brought me up close and personal with yet more corners of the county.

I said I've been photographing Lancashire for a long time. I should have added that I'm not tired of it yet. It may not have made me rich, but it's made my life richer.

Easegill Kirk, above Leck Beck

The valley of Beckerthwaite Beck, above Arkholme

Springtime, Over Kellet

Footbridge, Leighton Beck near Arnside

Train and Arnside Tower from Silverdale Moss

Moss on wall, Silverdale Moss

Silverdale from King William's Hill

The Kent Estuary from Jack Scout

Deepdale Pond, near
Yealand Conyers

Limestone pavement, Gait Barrows

Common toads near Hawes Water

Wild daffodils near
Jenny Brown's
Point

Salt marsh near Jenny Brown's Point

Sunset over Leighton Moss

Morecambe Bay from Warton Crag

Silverdale and the Coniston Fells from Warton Crag

Carnforth from Warton Crag

Carnforth Station

Fishing boat, Morecambe and the Coniston Fells

LR66

Eric Morecambe Statue,
Morecambe Promenade

The Midland Hotel, Morecambe

Mother and Child Sculpture, Morecambe

Standstone carving and St Patrick's Chapel, Heysham Head

Lancaster Castle, Priory Church and Coniston Fells

St George's Quay and the River Lune, Lancaster

White Cross, Lancaster

Lancaster from Castle Hill

Fireworks and train, Lancaster

Bridge, Crook O'Lune

Floods, Lune Valley

Evening, River Lune near Bull Beck

The Great Stone of Fourstones looking towards Gragareth, Whernside, and Ingleborough

The Hindburn Valley and Bowland Fells from Whitepits Lane

Snowman, Little Cragg

Evening, Little Cragg

Wolfhole Crag

The Shepherd's Church (Christ Church, Over Wyresdale)

Winter on the Marshaw Wyre

Valley of the Tarnbrook Wyre

Ward's Stone and Over Wyresdale

Sunset, Catshaw Greave, Hawthornthwaite Fell

Sheep on Harrisend Fell looking towards Clougha Pike

Mist, Over Wyresdale

Evening, Miller's House looking towards Whins Brow

Morning, Brock Bottom

Bleasdale and Beacon Fell

Paragliders, from Parlick

The Fleece Inn

Pink purslane, near Abbeystead

The Loud Valley and Bowland Fells from Jeffrey Hill

Clitheroe from Birdy Brow

Kitcham Hill and Ingleborough from Longbridge Fell

Autumn, Grize Dale near Scorton

Misty morning above Oakenclough

Memorial, Dunsop Fell

IN MEMORY OF

Sgt W R COVENEY
ROYAL AIR FORCE
P/O J M GILMER
NEW ZEALAND AIR FORCE
CRASHED 30.4.1940 DUNSOP FELL
1st Lt J E FIELDS
2nd Lt O CASTO
Sgt E E LYON
T/Sgt P MASSAGATTI
USA AIR FORCE
CRASHED 2.1 1945 BURN FELL
1st Lt H L PERRY
2nd Lt S L WHITE
USA AIR FORCE
CRASHED 26.1.1943 DUNSOP FELL
& BAXTON FELL
Sgt P STRUNIEWSKI
POLISH AIR FORCE
CRASHED 15.2 1945 BENTHAM

REST IN PEACE

North Lancashire Bridleway
Wood House Lane

North Lancashire Bridleway
Hornby Road

Dunsop Head

The Quernmore valley

Summit of Pendle Hill

14 %

Low gear
for 1/2 mile

Cyclist on Nick of Pendle

Inner basin, Glasson Dock

Bridge at Conder Green

Canal junction, near Galgate

Plover Scar lighthouse at the mouth of the River Lune

Tithebarn Basin, Garstang

Moorings, Lancaster Canal, Garstang

Bridge 66, Lancaster Canal

Mute swans, Lancaster Canal

Greenhalgh Castle, Garstang

Ducks by the River Wyre, Garstang

Autumn morning, Winmarleigh

Winter evening near Garstang

St Michael's on Wyre

Misty evening, Pilling

Subsidence, Union Lane, near Pilling

Old Fire Station, Singleton

Parlick from near Nateby

By Crawley's Dyke, Winmarleigh Moss

The Mount, Fleetwood

Hulk, Wyre estuary, near Fleetwood

Promenade, Cleveleys

Fireworks, Blackpool

The Windmill and old Lifeboat House, Lytham

St Anne's Sands

The Ribble Estuary looking towards Preston

Riversway Docklands, Preston

Lancaster Canal Tramroad Bridge, Preston

Stocks and St Anne's Church, Woodplumpton

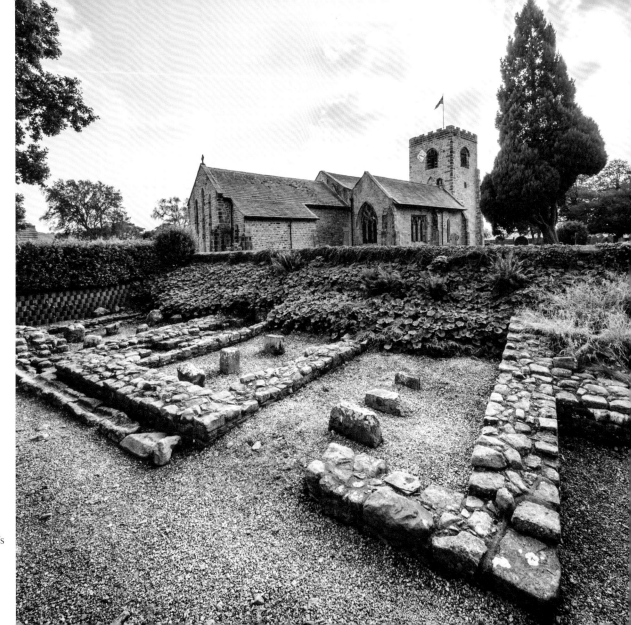

Roman granaries and St Wilfrid's
Church, Ribchester

The Ribble below Marles Wood

Confluence of Ribble and Hodder

Clitheroe Castle

The Ribble at Sawley

Pumpkins, Tarleton Moss

Greenhouses, Tarleton Moss

Mere Sands Wood

Corn Marigolds, Mere Lane, Rufford

River Yarrow and packhorse bridge, Croston

Rufford branch canal at Glover's Bridge, Burscough

Brussels sprouts, Clieves Hills, near Ormskirk

The Pennines from Clieves Hills

West Lancashire from Harrock Hill

Fairy Glen

Astley Hall, Chorley

Colne and Pendle Hill from Combe Hill

The Rooley Moor Road above Rossendale

The air of heaven is that which blows between a horse's ears

Mary Towneley MBE 1332 1935–2001 who conceived this monument and whose vision opened up this bridleway...

Mary Towneley Memorial beside the Penine Bridleway

Holden Vale near Haslingden

The Halo, Top o' Slate above Haslingden

Rivington Terraced Gardens

Belmont and the Penines from Winter Hill

Manchester and the Peak District from Winter Hill

Masts on Winter Hill

Healey Dell